THE FLYAWAY FIELDTRIP

Written & illustrated

BY: York Elvie

Dedicated to my favourit student, If I have one. You would know who you are,
And I would say, "Thanks for always being kind and having a laugh".

ROOM 102
SOLAR SYSTEM

It was the day of all days, the trip of all trips: Class 102 was going to a special place this year the airport! All the kids were excited, but one boy was more excited than the rest. His name was Dontay. Dontay loved the airport more than anyone else, he loved the ticket gate, the air traffic controllers, the tower, the airplanes but most of all, he loved the baggage trains.

As the class lined up in the hallway, Dakota ran to the front. She liked being line leader. But today everyone was so happy that no one minded who led the line as long as they were going to the airport.

"We're going to the airport!" shouted Dontay, almost jumping out of his skin with excitement. He stood next to his best friend Juliet, who always had a big smile and bouncy red hair.

Christie St
TTC
SUBWAY
CHRISTIE STATION
SUBWAY MAP

Everyone followed Miss R. and Lynda out of the school. The class was a busy bunch, so they needed two adults to manage them. Miss R. taught the kids, and Lynda helped keep an eye on them and their work.

Lynda looked at Miss R. and said, "Today is going to be busy, but so fun."

"It will be, I know it will." Miss R. replied trying to convince herself. She turned to Ely and asked, "Which way to the airport?"

Ely was a great navigator and knew the way. He'd even mapped the route out last night. "We walk down to Christie Station, then go east to Spadina Station, then south to Union Station, and take the UP Express all the way to the airport."

SPADINA
SP
To Miss R
Toronto Subway/RT
Yonge-University-Spadina
Scarborough RT
Bloor-Danforth
Sheppard
station   transfer   VIA Rail   GO Train
Finch
North York Centre
Sheppard-Yonge
Bessarion
Bayview
Leslie
Don Mills
Downsview
Wilson
Yorkdale
Lawrence West
Glencairn
Eglinton West
York Mills
Lawrence
Eglinton
Davisville
St. Clair
Summerhill
Rosedale
Castle Frank
Midland
McCowan
Ellesmere
Scarborough Centre
Lawrence East
Kennedy
Warden
Victoria Park
Main Street
St. Clair West
Dupont
Spadina
St. George
Bloor-Yonge
Sherbourne
Wellesley
College
Dundas
Queen
King
Union
Bathurst
Museum
Queen's Park
St. Patrick
Osgoode
St. Andrew
Bay
Kipling

And that's exactly what the class did. On the way there, Miss R. was so busy that she didn't hear Juliet calling her. "Miss R! Miss R! Miss R…!" Juliet sighed. "Oh well," she said, and went back to having fun with her friends.

Later, Miss R. found a note in her bag. On top, it said: To Miss R. She opened it and read it out loud.

Dear Miss R.,

I understand that you decided to take the class to the airport for a special trip. Though it may be wonderful and suitable for most, I feel that for me to benefit from a special trip, I must depart and go on my own adventure. I will be going to Jurassic Land. I'll meet you at Christie Station at 2:35 p.m. Enjoy your day.

Jason

"OH NO!" cried Miss R. "What are we going to do? We lost Jason! I think the trip is over."

Toronto Subway/RT
Yonge-University-Spadina
Scarborough RT
station   transfer   VIA Rail   GO Train
Finch
North York Centre
Sheppard-Yonge
Bayview
Bessarion
Leslie
Don Mills
Downsview
Wilson
Yorkdale
Lawrence West
Glencairn
Eglinton West
York Mills
Lawrence
Eglinton
Davisville
St. Clair
Summerhill
Rosedale
Bloor-Yonge
St. George
Spadina
Dupont
St. Clair West
Midland
McCowan
Ellesmere
Scarborough Centre
Lawrence East
Kennedy
Warden
Victoria Park
Main Street
Bathurst
Museum
Queen's Park
St. Patrick
Osgoode
St. Andrew
College
Wellesley
Dundas
Queen
King
Union
Kipling

"NOOOOOOOOOOOOO!" screeched Dontay.

"Wait a second, wait a second," said Lynda. "There's nothing we can do about Jason. Who's going into Jurassic Land to fight dinosaurs and look for Jason? Not me."

No one said a word because no one was going into Jurassic Land without Jason beside them. He was the only one who knew all the dinosaurs and how to stay safe around them. He might even be the only one who knew how to get there.

"And Jason is a responsible friend," added Bella. "He'll meet us at Christie Station like he said."

"You're both right," said Miss R. "He'll be fine. But I am going to have to talk to him about leaving to go on his own trip. Let's get to the airport!"

"Yay!" shouted the class all happy once again. And off they went.

CHECK-IN
→ Departures
AirCanada
West Jet
American
AirTransat
Sunwing

When they got to the airport, the kids were all smiles.

"What's that? What's that? What's that, Miss R.?" asked Ray, pointing to the giant dinosaur remains.

"That's a dinosaur fossil," Miss R. answered.

"Wow, it's so big," said Rose.

Everyone was quiet, probably thinking about Jason at Jurassic Land.

"Oh well," said Dontay. "Let's keep going. I'm not leaving this place until I see a cockpit and a baggage train."

The class knew there was no chance of changing Dontay's mind, so on they went.

A tour guide came up to them. "Hi, my name is Kate, and I'll be your guide for the day. Pearson Airport is a very busy place, so stay close to me at all times, or you're sure to get lost. Pearson Airport opened in 1939."

"That's when my mom was born," said Michael, who liked to exaggerate.

BAGGAGE ONLY
NO PASSENGERS
← GATES
CHECK-IN

"Okay, let's go see the check-in counter. This is where people check in. Look at all the different airline counters," Kate said.

"Air Canada, WestJet, American Airlines, Air Transat, Sunwing I know them all!" said Dontay excitedly.

"Now it's time to go behind the scenes." Kate looked very excited

"Where are we going, Kate?" asked Juliet.

"We're going to follow the path luggage takes to a Boeing 767." Kate replied.

The kids were so excited but not even half as excited as Dontay. His smile was so big it nearly ate up his whole face. The Boeing 767 was his favorite airplane in the entire world, and the only thing he liked more was baggage trains.

The class got weighed one at a time and then put on the conveyor belt for a ride. They went behind the counter and then down, down, down. **"WHOA!"** the class yelled as the conveyor belt went up and down, round and round, until Class 102 ended up in a heap on the floor of a big hangar.

BAGGAGE ONLY
NO PASSENGERS

"What a fun ride! Can we go again?" asked Sammy as the pile of students and teachers untangled themselves. At the bottom of the pile, Miss R. lay just a little flatter than she used to be.

She stood up and shook herself until she popped back to her regular size. "Ah, that's better. No thank you, Sammy.
I don't think I want to go on that ride again I don't like being as flat as a pancake."

Once the class was all straightened out, Kate continued the tour. "So when the bags get here, the workers load
them onto a baggage train."

Suddenly, two very big workers appeared and started tossing the class onto a baggage train. Once again, they were going for a ride! Miss R.'s head popped out from the bottom of the pile just in time to see Dontay scramble into the driver's seat before the worker did. Juliet was right beside him. She turned the key, and Dontay pressed the gas pedal all the way down. The bagage train lurched forward, with Lynda hanging onto the back like a flag flapping in the wind.

"DONTAY, SLOW DOWN!" Lynda shouted

Michael was surfing on the hood, while Dakota and Rose danced around trying to keep their balance. The rest were laughing and enjoying the ride. Ray had found his way to behind Juliet, calmly reading the baggage train manual. Miss R. was still too dizzy to move.

"DONTAY, SLOW DOWN!" Lynda Shouted again

The baggage train zoomed around the hangar doing loop-de-loops until Ray reached over, pulled the emergency brake, and turned the key. "That's too fast, Dontay."

The train came to a screeching halt. Lynda flew backward into the cart and landed on Sammy, Bella, and Ely. They turned into a ball of people and rolled right back onto Miss R. "Aww, this is just not my day," she muttered from the bottom of the pile.

Now that was a ride," said Michael." I can now say that I have lived, " said Dontay. "But I'm sorry, he shouldn't have left the keys in the ignition, then this wouldn't have happened."

Kate came running over to the group. "Well, that looked like fun! Most kids go over the ramp, though. Oh well, you missed it. It's time to go to the next part of the tour."

Dontay, Juliet, and Ray started to join the rest of the class. "I think we should end this trip now," said Miss R.

"Are you guys okay?" Dakota asked Lynda and Miss R

"Yeah, you don't look so well, " added Bella. Their hair was frizzy, their faces were pale, and their clothes were on backwards.

"You'll be fine," Kate said. "The tour is almost over."

Dontay's phone suddenly rang. It was Jason. Dontay crouched at the back of the baggage train so they could talk in private. Juliet was right beside him. "Hey Dontay, I'm in trouble. Can you come get me?"

"Where are you?"

"I'm still in Jurassic Land. Mr. Eivle is here. I freed all the dinosaurs from him, and now he's after me."

"That Mr. Eivle is always causing trouble. Send me the directions, and I'll get there as soon as I can. Remember to look up. "

Dontay hung up just in time to see the baggage train pull up to the Boeing 767 with the Air Canada symbol on its tail. He whistled. "It's beautiful."

The same two big workers came out of nowhere and started loading the class onto the plane, but not into the seats, underneath the plane, where all the luggage goes. Somehow, Dontay slipped away, and Juliet scampered with him.

They found their way to the cockpit. "Wow, I never thought I'd be here," Dontay said as he got ready to sit in the pilot's seat, staring at all the buttons.

They heard a noise and turned around. Ray was standing there. "What are you guys up to?" asked Ray.

"Well, I got a call from Jason. He needs our help," Dontay said.

"Okay, let's go" said Ray, sitting in the flight engineer's seat and opening the manual. Juliet slid into the co-pilot's seat. The class had just gotten into the cabin when Dontay jumped up, shut the cockpit door, and locked it.

"Dontay, you open that door right now!" Miss R. demanded. " I expect more from you, Juliet," she pleaded, but all she heard was Juliet's giggle through the door.

Dontay picked up the microphone. "This is your captain speaking. We'll be taking a short flight today. Please sit down, keep your trays up, and fasten your seatbelts." Ray pressed a bunch of buttons, and the engines roared to life.

"NOOOOOOOO!" cried Miss R. and Lynda at the same time.

"When things like this happen, I think it's best to just roll with it and put your seatbelt on," said Kate.

FLIGHT
MANUAL

Dontay sat back in the pilot's seat and started driving the plane with his co-pilot Juliet. In no time, they were in the air, though the take-off was pretty shaky. Miss R. looked like she didn't know what day it was, and Lynda looked like she'd seen a ghost.

Dontay spoke over the PA again. "Today we'll be flying over Jurassic Land. Please keep all hands and feet inside the vehicle. And Michael, could you come to the cockpit door, please?"

Miss R. was not pleased with this situation one bit.

Dontay gave Michael a plan to save Jason.

"We're here. Please stay in your seats," Dontay said.

The big 767 circled Jurassic Land until they saw Jason running down a hill toward a cliff that dropped down into icy water. Something was chasing him, it looked like a giant egg reflecting light… wait, no, it was the bald head of Mr. Eivle.

Jason was running out of space. Dontay brought the plane low, angling it to meet Jason at the cliff's edge.

"Now, Michael!" Dontay yelled through the speakers. Michael jumped out the back of the plane, harness attached, and dove through the air. At that moment, Jason jumped off the cliff and Michael caught him.

"Amazing," Miss R. said, watching out the window.

But Mr. Eivle wasn't so lucky. He leapt for the rope but was too late, Bella was already at the other end, pulling the two boys back into the plane.

Mr. Eivle plunged into the freezing water. the entire plane heard him scream. **"I HATE THE COLD!"** They flew back to the airport with the whole class together again.

Ray finished the manual and pressed a few buttons to lower the landing gear. Dontay and Juliet landed the plane safely with Ray's guidance. When they got off the plane Miss R. and Lynda kissed the ground.

"Thank you, thank you, thank you" they said with shaky voices.

Miss R. stood up, turned to the class and said, "I liked how you worked together today, but I don't know if we'll be going on another class trip again anytime soon."

9 781777 872434